ON LOVE

Also by Rita Baker

Born of Love

Of Breeding and Birth

My Dear Cousin Sadie

Victim of Circumstances (co-author)

On Love

A collection of poems
by

RITA BAKER

2nd Edition
Revised & Expanded

ADELAIDE BOOKS
New York / Lisbon
2022

ON LOVE

A collection of poems

By Rita Baker

Second edition / Revised & Expanded

Copyright © by Rita Baker

Cover design © 2022 Adelaide Books LLC

Published by Adelaide Books, New York / Lisbon

adelaidebooks.org

Editor-in-Chief

Stevan V. Nikolic

For any information, please address Adelaide Books

at info@adelaidebooks.org

or write to:

Adelaide Books

244 Fifth Ave. Suite D27

New York, NY, 10001

ISBN: 978-1-958419-32-8

Printed in the United States of America

In Memory
of Harry and our Everlasting Love

Contents

ON LOVE

Once you have loved and known that
      deep and exquisite pain,
Is there one who would not wish it back
      again, again and again?
Once you have tasted your first
      sweet, trembling, kiss,
Have hovered on the brink of ecstasy
      and perfect bliss,
Is there one who could bid their heart
      be forever still?
Or could turn from an embrace and
      never crave their fill?
Once you have loved and hungered
      for another
Have given your heart and lived for
      one another
Could you hold love but once to let
      it slip away?

Could you, when love was yours, not live
      in memory of that day?

SHADOWS

I live in the shadow
Of our love,
In the moments we shared,
Moments that will remain
Forever in my heart.
For nothing is lost
Once it has been had.
For it will live again,
To rise at my command.
Before once more tucked away
In the corners of my mind.
Waiting and waiting,
Awaiting my will.
You and me
Through all eternity.

DEAR HEART

I think of you both night and day
Of how we were together
Of how it was to be apart
        while longing to be with you.

Feelings don't die when life is gone,
Thoughts take on a life of their own,
And hope persists though life is done
        while longing stays forever.

Alone, yet I am not alone
Comforted by thoughts of you.
You cannot die if I live on,
        for as I live then so do you.

I see the ground in which you lie,
Stand by the grave my thoughts of you,
Remembering once so fine,
        when I was yours and you were mine.

IF I FAIL TO HEAR

If I fail to hear you it is
Because I fail to hear
What fails to interest me.
Your words become silent
Upon reaching my ears.
They are like clouds
In the sky
Drifting towards that
Unknown place in my mind
That surfs through the muddle
Of life's iniquitous
Bundle of inconsequential
Matter that eventually
Comes to rest
At my feet
And be trodden
Into the ground's
Dark earth never
To be resurrected
For future generations
To ponder over
And decide their worth.
For I have no worth

Except for what life
Delivers at my door
And too often
My door is shut
Too tight
To allow life to
Enter my domain.

Though I am poorer,
I fear,
For the lack of it.

FEAR

Fear is a dark veil
That shrouds the mind
And hides our sins
From the world around.

Fear is the enemy
Of love and hope
Of a soul that cowers
Beneath despair.

It haunts our thoughts
And drives emotion
To the edge of insanity.

Fear is the sieve
That filters life
Despite the living.

Fear is the enemy
Of enlightenment.
For without enlightenment
There is no fulfillment.

ON HIS BLINDNESS

He is blind without light
And sees with inner sight.
We met by chance
It took but one glance.
He sees my inner soul
And makes me feel whole.
Hears the tinkle in my laugh.
And takes strength from my staff.
Imagines the smile on my face
And believes in my grace.
He may be hesitant when he walks
But candid when he talks.
He thrives, needs no goal
He is complete, he is whole.
Sees more than I
With my seeing eye.
For I see but the shell
While he sees beyond the well.
And I hope I might one day be
As whole as to how he thinks of me.

WE WERE ONE

We were one beneath the moon
And we were one beneath the stars.
We were one under the sun
And were one in the grass.
We were one on the hilltop.
We were one by the seashore.
We were one in the forest
And we were one in the sand.

We were one in a bubble
Of the body and the mind.
Were one in each other's eyes
And one in each other's hearts.
We were one in every way
From the moment that we met.
Were one forever in life.
Shall be forever in death.

ON DEATH

I walk like a shadow of the night.
Yet still, I hear the birds once in flight.
And my heart beats as a dreamer's might.

Am I now dead, or am I alive?
Who calls the tune so I might survive?
Is there a path by which to thrive?

Is death too near, has it ever been?
Is life more than it may seem?
Are hopes still with me as once so keen?

Hope cannot live on when we are gone.
It's gone forever, as once upon.

What means life tween here and passing?
Is death life's final test surpassing?

TO HARRY

In loving you I've learned full well
The measure of my constant heart.
That I have never loved before
Not in whole, or indeed, in part.

I know the strength of your embrace.
I know the comfort of your hand.
I know the meaning of our love
Goes far beyond the wedding band.

I have no dream where you have no part.
I have no thought where you have no place.
No hope that does not enfold you.
I have no life but by your grace.

Love is not love that does not last
Or alters with the tricks of life.
So, come what may, until my death,
I am, my love, your constant wife.

MEMORIES

How can he be gone
When my heart won't let him go?
When I see his face
In every waking moment?
When I feel his breath
On every summer breeze?
Or hear his voice
In every love song written?

How can he be gone
When his touch still lingers
Placed once upon my arm?
While lips still warm on mine
Retrace thoughts of his love?
How can he be gone
If I will not let him go?

SEASCAPE

Forward, pounding, breaking waves.
Back retreating meeting waves.
Like a mountain riding high
Rolling and arched against the sky
It's back again towards the shore
Repeating rhythms as before.
All blue and green and foaming white
Exiting with its powerful might.

Then further on along the beach
Where width limits the water's reach
It inches its way up the sand
To hurry back from the land.
A ritual dance performed with grace
Hugging the shore in a quick embrace
Like a bond you cannot sever
An affair that lasts forever.
One moment heaving beating wild
The next moment gently swaying mild
A fury when the wind whipped and blown
Calm peaceful when left alone.

TIME

When times passes
Life passes.
When dreams fail
Hope fails.
When love ends
Hearts wither.
When a man stands straight
The world bends.
When light dulls
Eyes dim.
When beauty conquers
Man is lost.

RANDOM THOUGHTS

Fear is all-consuming.
Hope is all illuming.
Doubt is all conflicting.
Certainty is all uplifting.
Hate is winter's wining.
Love is summer's shining.
Greed is liberty dying.
Giving is pleasure sighing.

Love is life
And life is love.
I have no dreams
But yours in me.
The door stood open
And you departed.
If I had closed it
Would you still be?

The dying embers gleam
In the flickering candlelight.
Shadows on the wall dance
Growing taller before
Receding out of sight.
The warm breath of night
Empowers my thoughts
And have you with me
Dancing in the embers light.

A PRICE

To everything
There is a price
A price to giving.
A price to taking.
A price to loving.
A price to hating.
A price to doing.
A price to failing.
A price retreating.
A price advancing.
A price to living.
Pay it.
The payments stop
AT DYING.

TAKE THE TIME

Take the time to look and see
Grass growing, a leafy tree,
Rivers running deep and clear
On their way from there to here.

The bird in a tree that sings,
The beauty of their spreading wings,
The sails of a ship at sea
Blown by winds we cannot see.

The joy of a lover's glance,
The magic steps of his dance.
The rhythm of a beating drum,
Its notes for the world to hum.

A baby in the mother's arms
Its teething she alone calms.
Wonders of simply being
Of joys and hopes each day seeing.

MELANCHOLY

Melancholy, haunted brain,
Terrors of a mind in pain.
Feelings flitting to and fro,
Passions running high then low.
Tears to spring but un-sprung yet,
Maddening folly, then regret.
Laughing, crying, never still.

Loving, hating, lack of will.
Backward, forward, broken sleep,
Emotions ever running deep.
Hurting loved ones with intent,
Pining, whining, remorse bent.
And the ever-present fear
Of losing all you hold most dear.

ON LIFE

It comes, it goes.
For a while, it stays.
A silent memory
In repose.

Who will recall
On one such day,
Moments in time
Before the fall,
That we two were,
For a brief age,
Until once more
We left the stage.

If life is fleeting,
Then so is time.
Until, my love,
Our next meeting.

PROOF

When I am gone what proof
To say that I was here,
That I cried with my friends,
Laughed with my enemies,
That my light was strong
And my dark hidden.

What proof will tell of me
That once I had loved
And had been loved,
That lived in the sunshine
And wished upon the moon,
That I conquered
And been conquered.

That I had been driven
And had taken the bait,
That my will was strong
And never broken,
What proof will there be
Once covered by earth.

WITH YOU IT WAS ALL

My thoughts were simple
My dreams untraveled.
My hopes not wanting
My choice unravelled.
My life was yours
And yours was mine.
Your kiss was the breath
Of a dream come true.
Your touch the magic
Of a drummer's beat.
Your eyes the depth
Of the ocean's floor.
And your smile the light
Of the morning sun.
I could not want more,
Our life was one.
Our hopes delivered,
Without exception.
I was yours and you were mine.
Without redemption.

FASTER-FASTER

It appears the older
I get the faster
Time flies.
Slow down.
Slow down,
I cry in vain.
But it seems
No tears I shed
Will make time
Take the slower lane.

WORDS

Words are like
shadows on a wall,

Creating images,
that is all.

Put not your trust
in words alone,

Lest to be sure,
they are your own.

LOST LOVE

I knew from his eyes
     what was impending.
Our romance, our love
     was ending.
Like rivers flowing
     out to sea,
For one brief moment
     love touched me.
Drifting like
     a log of wood,
Entangled for a while
     we stood.
Then swiftly carried
     on its way,
As if regretting
     more delay.
Now in the distant light
     it fades,
Like purple to pink
     through the shades.
And I am left
     far behind,
A memory in
     a wandering mind.

IF

If
He was to walk in now
I would run straight to him.

I would take his hand in mine
And sit me down beside him.

Place my head on his shoulder,
Close my eyes and enjoy
The splendour of a love surpassing.

He'd then place an arm around me
And draw me closer to him.

And there we'd sit together,
Wrapped In the magic of our love.

If
He was to walk in now.

HEAVEN OR EARTH

Is there a space between heaven
and earth where we may meet?
Is there a drifting cloud that
dare might take us there?
Is there a purpose to our being
less here and more there?
Drifting in that space between
before decisions made,
To be or not to be?

Who makes that decision,
if not I, not thee?
For certain, it must be
HE.

THE RAVAGES OF WAR

I remember the war.
The streets dark,
Black curtains drawn.
The droning sound of
Enemy planes.
Searchlights scanning,
Flack dropping.
Ack-ack cracking
While bombs were falling.

The trembling walls,
The floors that give.
The ceilings downed.
Death all around.
The cry of a baby.
A dead mother's arms
Still clinging
As she clung before.

The fires that scorched.
The smoke that choked.
A missing arm,
A missing leg.
The shock in the eyes
Of a face no more.

Oh yes, for sure.
I remember the war.

LETTER TO MY HUSBAND

If I tremble at your touch,
Or my heart melts with your kiss,
It's so much more than my love for you,
It's that you make it possible
To be forever in love.

Your gentleness is as that of a
Summer breeze rustling the leaves
With whispered words of love.
Tender as the flower that cups
The morning dew.
Your strength is that of
A windblown wave
Rushing to the shore with
Its roaring passion.
Strong as the current that
Jealously pulls back.

You are so special to love,
And in so doing I too
Am touched by that same hand
That touches you.

You have given me,
In your constant love,
The coveted gift

Of youth eternal.
For all that may
Be left unsaid,

I say to you now, beloved,
There could never be another.

A love such as ours
Comes but once.
Served by time to
Strengthen that love.

I could not want or ask
For else in life.
And I am left with
But one last wish,
To lie beside you in
The deep cool earth,
Life's final bond of
Love everlasting.

NOW HE IS GONE

He is gone.
The sun's rays
No longer shine so bright.
While the moon's glow dims
Wrapped in a shroud of clouds,
Taking flight in the night.

Where is the strength I knew
     with him by my side?
What happens to hopes lost,
     gone with his passing?
Are they placed in a box
     hidden from view?
Or tucked inside
     and battened down,
No more to come to light?

A FOOL'S GOLD

A fool's gold.
A love grown cold.
A waste of life.
The workers' strife.

What happened
To something
Good to say,
Of hope, of love
Passing your way?

Who can tell
What is to be?
We can but hope
A light to see.

IF LIFE IS DEATH

What is this hatred in my heart?
Tell me, God.
For if in hating I cannot love,
Teach me then to pity.

Teach me to live.
Without love no man lives.
He, who is filled with wrath,
 dies already dead
And lives forever after.
So come, sweet death,
What good is life
If life is death?
I wish it were
That I was dead and living.

(First poem written at the age of 12)

HE

You smiled,
     my heart stood still.
You spoke,
     and bells were heard.
You looked,
     and I was lost.
You touched,
     your strength was known.

And arms
Around me folded.
At one
We were together.
You were mine, I knew.
And I was yours.
Forever.

SHE

Her laugh was tinkling,
            I was told.
Her smile was gentle,
            I was told.
She was filled with life,
            I was told.
Loved by everyone,
            I was told.
Her warmth was real,
            I was told.
A joyous being,
            I was told.
She played piano,
            I was told.
Violin as well,
            I was told.
Her father's favorite,
            I was told.
She held me but once,
            I was told.
And shed tears of love,
            I was told.

AGE

The streets now damp and cold.
And the night's chill now bold.
Trees barely display a leaf
Awaiting autumn's brief
Show of changing times
As season upon season climbs.

Lost, too, the spring of our days
As we adapt to autumn's ways.
What happened to the golden years?
Why are my eyes now filled with tears?
Will next year ever come again
For me?
Should I still be?

YOUTH

When I was young,
It seemed to me,
All gifts from heaven
Would forever be.
The honeyed flowers,
The bumblebees,
The sun that shines,
The leafy trees,
The grass that grows,
Star studied streams,
Meandering through
The country greens.
And love that remains
Forever true.

But when love may leave,
Then comes despair.
A lover's tryst
Is seen nowhere.
A heart that breaks,
A world that takes.
But hope must remain
Or all is pain.

HE granted hope,
To keep us sane.

LIFE

Take the time to look and see
The grass that grows, a leafy tree.
Rivers running deep and clear
On their way from there to here.
The bird in a tree that sings,
The beauty of its spreading wings.
The sails of a ship at sea
Blown by winds we cannot see.
The joy of a lover's glance,
The magic steps of his dance.
A baby in the mother's arms,
The cries she alone calms.
The wonder of simply being,
Of joys, hopes, each day seeing.
And we are in wonder left.
All is hope. Nothing bereft.

OF FEAR AND HOPE

Fear is all-consuming.
Hope is all illuming.
Doubt is all conflicting.
Certainty is all uplifting.
Hate is winter's wining.
Love is summer's shining.
Greed is liberty dying.
Giving is love's sighing.

WHEN I LEAVE

If I were to leave tomorrow,
  Is there a place for me to borrow?
  Is there a spot that I once knew
    Where life may resume before it blew?
    And pasts recede as if they won't die
      If I were to leave on tomorrow's high?
        Who'd then bear witness to my being?
          Who'd then tell of my hopes of seeing?
          Of the joys and sorrows of my days?
            Of loves that happened along with life's ways?

The fire in me once burned bright
And I was caught in its heated light.
Was that truly me, or was it not?
Tell me for I have forgot
Am I a figment of a dreamer's sleep
Or a page unread in a book I keep?

FORMS

Forms. Forms. Forms.
Forms for everything.
Forms for school.
Forms for college.
Forms for work.
Forms for marrying.
Forms for birth.
Forms for divorce.
Forms for hospital.
Forms for living.
Forms for…Hm!
No forms for that!
Forms for when I die.
Who will fill out that form?
Someone else, thank heaven.

POETRY

What kind of poetry
Am I writing?
Some rhythm, some rhyme.
Some nothing at all.

What kind of poetry
Am I writing?
Taken from the old,
Taken from the present.

What kind of poetry
Am I writing?
Are they true
Poetic words,
Or inner thoughts
To be expressed?

What kind of poetry
Am I writing?
Words that touch the soul,
Words that touch the heart?

What kind of poetry
Am I writing?
If they are, indeed,
Poetic at all.

INNER THOUGHTS

Which door to open?
        Which door to close?
Life is uncertain
        From head to toes.
Which road to cross?
        Which path to take?
Life is a battle
        Or a piece of cake
Whose words to listen
        Whose words to doubt?
Life is confusing.
        What is it about?
My head's in a whirl,
        What's true, what's fake?
How do I know
        Which mud to rake?
Perhaps tomorrow
        I will gather more.
Perhaps tomorrow
        I will know the score.

AGE (1)

Is there no poetic
    justice left?
Am I getting old?
What once was,
    is now not.
And I am wandering
A desert of sand and stone
    remembering.

What if I speak?
Will the sand hear?
Will the stones cry out
when poetic words
Leave my lips
to an audience
Of captive pathing?
Or will my feet
just stumble
On uneven ground
as I try to find
My way around?

WHO

If I were not me,
Who would I like to be?
Shakespeare, Oh woe is me.
A burden too great to be.
Milton, Oh heavens no.
My sight could never be
To see as well as he.
Atlas, the world's a heavy sack
To carry on my back.
Einstein, perhaps.
With mathematics in my lap.
Think he, I better not had to be
And so, after all,
Who could I possibly be
But me?

TRUTH

People are not always what they seem.
Their words are not always what they mean.
And the truth lies somewhere in-between.

Are their words naught but confection
Arranged so for their protection?
Is fear a part of their persona?
Without truth, there is no honor.

It's hard to know another's feeling.
What's in their mind, why it is reeling?
I pity those not forthcoming.
What fears they hold yet up-coming.

Time is a stranger to their thinking
That passes swiftly in a blinking.
But time, that healer of all things.
And fear, as in hope, still has wings.

THEE AND ME

How sad are we
      that have no base.
Who wander through
      the human race
Without direction
      or time wanting.
To hide away
      our tears haunting.
In fear of letting
      others see
Who we are or
      meant to be.
In a selfish world
      of thee and me.

TICK TOCK

For everything
There is a time.
Then is time not
A passing thing?
Perhaps, maybe,
Let us see.
Let's do a count
Of you and me.

A time to be born and
A time to die.
A time to laugh and
A time to cry.
A time for giving and
A time for taking.
A time for you and
A time for me.
A time to see the
Flowers of spring.
And winter's snow and
Robins that sing.

And time is everything,
If, indeed,
There is such a thing.

WITHOUT FEAR

A child has no fear of dying.
Of leaving this world unseen.

But while the years' entrances,
So fear advances,
And time is the enemy
Of age arriving.

What about it do we fear?
What secrets unknown,
That mark life's passing?
What is there to fear,
If we know not what allays?
Perhaps not knowing
Is what we fear,
Not the dying days.

SOLOMAN
MY GRANDFATHER'S TREES

Trees stand tall in his orchard
Their branches heavy with fruit.
Rosy apples, blushing red
Waiting to be picked by gentle hands,
That lovingly touch their ripened bloom.
Bite into an apple tart and sweet,
Let their flavor capture your senses.
Crush them by invading teeth
Let their juice drizzling on the tongue
Remind you of heaven's gift.

Then all too soon the orchard's bare,
Their produce stored in cardboard boxes
To be delivered everywhere
To those in wait for their arrival.
People who have never known
The true taste of an apple
Fresh picked homegrown.

MACHINES OF WAR

Night after night they invaded the sky
Machines of war dropping their load.
Bombs whistling down from on high,
Windows shattering, walls trembling,
Ceilings crashing and
Shrapnel dismembering.

Arms missing, legs broken,
Unseeing eyes set
In faces un-woken.
Nowhere to hide,
Nowhere to run,
From the terrors of
The invading Hun.

But we were resilient,
Our fears fighting back.
If he thought he had us,
A fuss did we lack.
We stood firm and bold,
And strengthened our hold.
It was win or lose.

We were ready to choose.
And we chose not to die
Of those bombs from the sky.
He had met his match
Like no other he knew.
And night after night
We came through.

Determined again
To fight the fight.

TIME

Time passes slowly
When we are young.
We cannot wait for it
. To leave and again come.

But time used cannot
Return once more.
It is gone as in before.
Young or old it is briefly
For a while ours
Like the earth
And its show of flowers.

If the young waste it,
They know no better.
But do we, the elders,
Know much more?
We waste it
On a larger scale,
On useless hopes
To no avail.

Creatures of habit,
We never learn.
But hope is so
Deeply driven
As seen through
A glass given
To drink at will,
Life's tempting fill.

MY BELOVED

If I could press his lips on mine
        once more.
Or feel his arms about me
        once more.
What heaven would I enter!
To see him, to touch him, be with him
        once more.
But time that passes
        comes not again.
Perhaps in memory
        on a certain day.
But memory withers
        as with time.
And comes not again.
        And comes not again...

A LITTLE SHOP

There is a little shop
            around the corner.
It sells the prettiest things.

Well-loved it says,
            by the prettiest girls.
Buy now, it says,
            our clothes have wings.
I often pass by and
            look in the window.
Wondering to step in.

Should I yes
            or should I not?
So many lovely things!

But to enjoy
            another's dresses.
Would I yes or would I not?

But well-loved, it says,
            and so, why not?

PIE IN THE SKY

Have you ever wished
For the impossible?
Join the hopeful club.

How does that lyric go?
Wishing will make it so.
If you think to believe it,
Then who knows what may be.

Dreams can come true
And wishes often do.
The trick is belief
The forerun to hope.
So climb that slippery slope
And who knows what you find.

THE DICTIONARY

There is a dictionary for everything.
A dictionary for meaning,
A dictionary for rhyme.
But who uses a dictionary
For rhyming all the time?
They have broken the rules
Of poetry.
They have broken the rules
Of line.
They have broken so many rules
And left very little sign
Of a verse as well produced
As a canter of the finest wine.

OUR TIME

We didn't waste a second
of our time together.
We were bound,
Firm, and strong
With love enduring.
In-love for the length of
time it takes to get to know,
To understand what we were
to each other.
To be at one forever.

Our love never wavered,
And I am as much in love with him now,
As I was with him in life.
How could I look upon another's face,
Or feel another's touch
When my thoughts always
Turn to him and the miracle
Of what we shared
In those destined days
Of love.

If true love comes but once
I have had mine once.
And I cannot want
or wish for more.
For love everlasting
is everlasting.

DO YOU WEEP

Do you weep when summer's ended,
To see the brown creep along
the petals of a rose?
Or the drooping of a leaf
getting ready to fall,
After bursting forth in
a blaze of glory,
After last winter's long
and frigid sleep?
Do you weep when packing
away that shear and flimsy
Dress in a trunk along with
memories of the warmth
Of a summer's day?

Do you weep for a face
upturned towards the sun?
Feeling the warmth
of its sparkling ray
Wash the dull of winter away?
Do you weep or, as I, now rejoice
in the splendor of
The season in giving
Knowing that life is
Worth the living?

LIFE'S PATH

Life passes swiftly
In the blink of an eye.
Like a star in the sky
Life is here then gone
Losing its glitter
When passing from sight.
Not to be seen again
By day or night.

It matters not
Whether you were here
And then not.
It matters only
How your time was spent.
What gifts of yours were lent
To future generations
Before they too, went.

Life is temporary,
We are contemporary.
For a very short while
We are here, then not.
And hopefully,
Not to be forgot.

CERTAINTY AND DOUBT

There was a time in youth that seemed to me
All gifts from heaven would forever be
The birds that sing, the April showers,
The summer sun, and the honeyed flowers.
Nothing would come to pass, only remain,
No losses would be had, only gain.

I did not doubt my future life,
I would be a mother and a wife.
I knew for certain there would be love
And that God was in his heaven above.
All was hope without doubt and confusion,
Eternal life without death's intrusion.

But youth gives way to age and so to trust.
Certainty is shared with doubt, so we must
Learn not all is ours to have and to keep,
Eternal life becomes an eternal sleep.

FEAR

What is it we fear most,
Is it life or death?
We know what life is,
Its upturns and downturns,
Its pains and pleasures,
Its hopes and disappointments,
Its desires and regrets.
But what is death
If not the unknown,
The uncertain,
The frightening?
Of what are we afraid
If God's hand is
In everything?
In all we think,
In all we feel.
If death is but a
Part of life,
Lived then gone.
It surely must have been
Intended and woven
For his delight.

TAKE THE TIME

Time is not exclusive,
It embodies all.
Giving time to think,
Giving time to do
What we've wanted to.

Yet often it is squandered
On daily trivial schemes,
Wasting what is given
Of mine and your dreams.

Strange we should waste it
Knowing what the tally.
Life is not a rally,
Or a game to pursue.
Life has an intention
Of hopes and love's mention,
With no wrong to do.

All is not fair game.
It is not a win or lose.
It must be what we choose.
And we must choose
To win the fight,
And do what is right
For future generations.
Leaving them to cope
With a world full of hope.

I HAVE

I have seen the sun rise,
      and seen it set.
I have swum in rivers
      icy with cold.
Walked over hills
      of forest green.
Sunk my feet
      in the dust of sand.
Paddled in the dancing waves
      my toes to feel their lick.
Braved the strong winds that
      colored my cheeks,
That blew my hair,
      that made me gasp.
I have lived and loved
      and have been loved.
Have known the feel of
      an unborn babe.
Have weathered storms
      that rise and wain.
And cursed the torment
      of a befuddled brain.

I have known the joy to give
        and the joy to take.
The joy of sleep
        and then to wake.
Enjoyed the man
        my heart was given.
Enjoyed his love,
        to me driven.

Have enjoyed my life
and am thankful for it.

Oh yes, indeed,
I've surely lived.
I was a mother and a wife.

KIDS

I no longer wish
To see him.
Will a letter do?
We spent the summer
Together.
Will a brief note do?
There were times of
Kissing.
A card perhaps.
We spoke shy words of love.
A phone call, maybe.
He gave me his school badge.
So confusing.
Oh, there is a mother's call.

Good. Oh, who cares,
Not at twelve, after all.

DREAMS

I had such thoughts of thee and me,
And what my future life might be
When I was young and full of dreams.

I saw what might be laid before me
And with whom it was or might be.
Is our life just thus, made of schemes?

Perhaps it's more the dreamer in me
Wishes to see what there may be.
Perhaps nothing is what it seems.

But hope, there must be hope in me
Else what am I, or who to be?
Moons die cold if not filled with dreams.

MY DAYS

I sit, in the twilight of my years,
Empty, as a vessel drained.
Yet hope is ever with me still
And wishes abundant yet to fill.
Maybe not fulfilled quite as was,
But in remembrance if no more.
I've lived my life, cannot be sore.
Love was realized. I had it all.
Now I pray to live in peace.
Content to leave
When I hear the call.

MY WORLD

On a day like today
With a warm sun glowing,
And a soft breeze blowing,
I am drifting on a
Single cloud, being, seeing
The world from afar.
And what I am seeing
Is nature's love.
Animals roaming wild and free,
People dashing, a place to be,
Mountains ranging high and low,
Fields of green and rivers that flow,
Seas of dark and seas of blue,
Waves that rise before they fall.
A world, it seems, embracing all.

But whose dream does He deny?
For what purpose to so defy.
Those on the wretched side.
Are they not of human worth?
An accident perhaps of birth
Or of a purpose to be defined
And seen but once at low tide.

MY TRUE LOVE

I feel his presence all about me.
I feel his love all around me.
He is still with me, in our home,
In my dreams, in my life, by my side.
His photos stare back at me
From every corner of the room.
I see his face, I feel his glow.
He has never left
And I cannot let him go.
I go to the cemetery
And stand by his grave.
But he is not there
In the way that I
Feel him inside.
I know he awaits
My return back home.

I knew his love and know it still.
He knew my love and my strong will
And he gave me all of his
As I gave him all of mine.
I fear not death as before
For I know now
There will be more.

SOMETIMES

Sometimes, in bed at night,
Vacant of all emotion,
No thoughts inside my head,
The scent of you comes creeping
As though beside me in bed.

And my heart would uplift,
And my soul would be at peace,
And I would sleep content,
Waking with the morning light
As if you were with me through the night.

MY LIFE

I was never a wild one
Always level-headed.
Still lived with a passion.
And loved in my fashion.
But love is an emotion
That life has intended.
An emotion to thrive.
To keep the world alive.
Never meant to deny
Or to live on the edge
But to give and to give,
Making certain we live.

DREAM

I had a dream
I wished it to come true.
A dream of many
Of me and you.
But dreams don't come true
Except with the willing
Of me and you.
And once again
I am with you
To feel your touch.
And my dreams come true,
If by so much.

WHY

He did not introduce me
To a friend standing by.
I wondered why.
Did I have no standing
In his world or mine?
Was I not love's child
Or a stranger in his eye?
Was I so unseemly
He thought to hide the fact?
In what defense was his act?
It made me feel like nothing
Unwanted and of woe.
And my heart bled, my spirit low.

But somehow, my strength unlost,
I held my head up high.
It was his lie, not mine.
No purpose to define.
I had no need of him.
It was he who chose that line.
A line he chose to cross.
It was his loss, not mine.

CHANCES

What are the chances
 That life enhances
  As life goes trundling on.
   There's much debating
   As we stand waiting
    As in once upon.
     There is no ruling,
      Nor much fooling
       Once here, we're ever gone.

So take it easy,
 Nice and breezy,
  While time goes marching on.

TO MY BELOVED

We weren't meant to be apart.
So how come you're not with me?

Who decreed we should
No longer be together?

By what right were you taken
Before I, not to be
Together forever?

How long is forever?
How long before we
Are together once more?

How long before I
Can touch your face,
See your smile, hear your voice?

How long before I lie
At peace with you?

LOGIC

What logic is there to life?
What reason, if we are to pass
Out of sight and out of mind?
Here for a moment then gone forever.
All ties made but to sever.

What logic is there to life?
One moment of happiness,
And one moment of strife?
Moments, nothing more.
Not even counted.
Nothing as before.

JOSEPH

My Grandfather

The chill that swept the room came with his death.
His flesh once warm and vital now lay cold.
I pressed my lips against his stony cheek.
Never again would I hear his voice speak.

Still I hear his echo from ages past.
I hear the laughter in his gentle tone.
I still can hear the stories he once told.
And how for me they made the world unfold.

He gave me hope and taught me the love of man.
He taught all flesh is flesh and comes from one.
He had so much to teach and I to learn.
He loved mankind and was loved in return.

When I regret the passing of those years,
Then I recall how much he gave to me.
A life made richer just to have known him.
I am fulfilled. This is what I owe him.

A MAN NAMED HARRY

He went through life
Full steam ahead,
He knew no moderation.
He rode the waves,
He whipped the wind.
He had no hesitation.

Was black or white,
No compromise,
A mathematic equation.
The line was straight,
His word was true,
Without moral invasion.

Was mild, yet strong.
Not weak but kind.
A man for each occasion,
He spoke with force,
Emphatic moved,
Without the threat of persuasion.

A SIMPLE SOUL

I wish I were a simple soul
With simple tastes and simple needs.
Know nothing of the world about,
Nor in my God have any doubt.

I envy the small village life,
Nestled amid the rolling hills.
Protected from the city's race,
Safe with your quieter, slower pace.

Here the strife is for yellow gold,
The riches of the city kind.
We rush and push to play our game,
And we call it progress by name.

Your riches far exceed them all,
The country and the sweeter air.
You savor and enjoy your time.
No panic for the upward climb.

Your lives are lived with dignity
Of knowing who and what you are.
Your place on Earth is guaranteed,
Father to a son, an ancestral deed.

REVOLT REBEL

The air we breathe, the ground we toil
Everything we have we spoil.
Food is doused with chemical sprays,
Waste is dumped in our waterways,
Or buried in the earth somewhere,
Nothing we do is done with care.

The stage for cancer is well set,
Fifty, fifty is the bet.
Why don't we revolt and rebel?
Instead, we quietly go to hell.
Enough, enough, we must cry.
Who then, if not we, must try
To end the quest that is for wealth.
There is no substitute for health.
Let us not commit genocide.
No toxic waste, no pesticide.

SPEAK UP

Let us work to return that vital spark
When the world once again will be a park.
Why must birds fly
Among trees that die?
Only together can we work at length.
Only together will our voice have strength.
Let us speak, be heard.
Let us say the word.
Say no to the fumes that invade our air.
Say no to those who would dump without care.
No, no, no to all
Who heeds not this call.
No, we cannot wait till there is no choice
So rise up, rise up, and shout in one voice.

HERITAGE

Man should hide his head in shame.
The spewing of the motor car,
The toxics down our drain
Or hidden neath the land or sea.
Can do nothing but defame
The human race and its kind.
For there must be laid the blame.

What will we leave those who follow?
What expectations will they have?
What quality to find?
What air to breathe, what food to eat?
Promises that ring hollow?
Is that all that we will leave?
And waste in which to wallow?

A KINDER WAY

Why must we have nuclear power?
Why make our future bleak?
We know they're not safe, we know they leak.
Why must they spoil our days,
Our weeks, our months, and all our years?
These are not unfounded fears.
A kinder way please, a kinder way.
Protect our land, our race.
We want to be able to look
Our future in the face.

A TREE

There is a tree
That's standing free,
All its limbs outstretched.
Green leaves endow
Every bough
Against the sky etched.

Then sounds the drum,
Winter's to come
Every branch to bare.
The leaves turn gold
With the cold.
There is no sight more fair.

TO LOVERS EVERYWHERE

Love comes never too early
And never too late.
It's the vision that inspires us,
The twist that seals our fate.
The world becomes softer,
The sun much brighter.
The grass becomes greener,
The snow much whiter.
Hope resides in our hearts
And dreams fill our minds.
The kind that lives forever
In the resting place it finds.

SIMPLICITY

I love simplicity in a poem,
For therein lies the truth
Nothing hidden
By words of
Tortuous complication.
While bearing only
The fruit of
My imagination.
Words must touch
The heart or be
Left unsaid.
Words have an
Effect on all
To be awakened
By their sounding
Call.

ONCE MORE, MY LOVE

If I could see his face once more,
Touch his cheek as before,
Brush a kiss on his lips,
Caress his brow with fingertips,
Such heaven there would be,
Such joy there'd be for me.

But memories will have their life,
The time I was his wife,
When my love was so bold,
Ours to be lived and to be told.
Feelings up to the sky,
Forever running high.

YOURS

My heart is wild
with imagination.
My eyes are deep
with fascination.
My thoughts are fueled
with trepidation.
And I am yours
in anticipation.

LESS THAN NOTHING

How come my heart is full of hope
When I see doubt all about me?
By whose measure are we given
That by which all man is driven?
Can love be the secret weapon
That drives us with impunity?
Or are we all but puppets in unity
In the hands of an uncaring?
Are we in control of our fate
Or is fate open to debate?
What is our life if at the end
We have naught to give
And naught to lend.

SEASHIPS

Winds do whip
And ships lack gain
When the ocean roars
Like a lion in pain
And fury whips
Like a sea gone rogue
With mountainous waves
For sailor's graves
And all that sail
Upon that sea
Are a certainty
To forever be
Part of natures
Destiny
Then comes a day
When seas are calm
And ships roll gently
Free of harm.

WITH MY LOVE

I live in memory
Of our being
In our times of joy
Our moments of love
Of passion unsurpassed
My heart I gave freely
And you gave me yours
Yet with your passing
I hold it still
For love that's true
Endures forever
And I am still yours
And you are still mine.

WITH YOU

I close my eyes
And I am with you.
My arms about me
I dance
And I am with you.
I sleep
And I am with you.
Death cannot
Keep us apart.
If tomorrow I die
I shall be with you.

MY ONE LOVE

What heals my heart,
If not thoughts of you.
If I still live
It's in my love for you.
You haunt my dreams,
Occupy my days,
Fill me with hope
That once again
I shall be one
With you to wander
Through eternity.
I am nothing
Without your love.
I am nothing
Without you.

HOPE DIES NOT

My heart once free to brave the wind
My heart once free to ride the waves
My heart once mine, once so free
To live and love and so to give.

Remaining embers that once lived
Inside a shell that once was mine
Is now thrown to every corner
To find what was and now is.

A world bereft of he who was
But hope dies not when love's not dead
For death is but the beginning
Of the more that is to come.

Life may be short and death too long
But love lives on forever.

ANNIE WHO GIFTED ME MY LIFE

I live in the present
With my thoughts in the past.
It was a lovely past
Filled with love, joy, and hope
It was a life given
By the woman who gave me life.
My life, in place of hers.
A weight hard to bear when
 I think of what she lost
And what I gained in place.

There is no way
 To make amends
What is past is past
And the best I can do
Is not to waste what was given
For there would lie the cruelty
Of a life lost
When a life was given.
I can but give thanks
And do my very best

But I think of her
Every day of my living
I see her face beside
My bed, staring at me
From a photo taken
Upon her engagement
An engagement unknown
That would end with her parting

Her life, her love, her leaving
While I am left grieving.

It is what she gave me
What she left for me to live
Not to waste what was given
But to live in her place
And to make of it what she
Would have wanted me to make
And this I write to her
For all the world to see
And to know who she was
And what she means to me.

IF THERE IS NO SUCH THING AS TIME

If there is no such thing as time
Then what is it we are spending?
While it is easy to understand
There is no such thing as time
Where do light and dark
Fit into life on earth
Be there no such thing as time.
So what is all the fuss
Between birth and death

If there is no such thing as time
There is no such thing as age
As we spend this
Abnormality called time
That makes our TIME
Non-existent in a world
Of no time.
And so, my friends
Make the most of what
You yet may spend
Until you and I
Into the dark descend.

About the Author

I am a novelist, creating stories out of thin air, yet not thin air, since each story is a part of my life, and a part of me has been aching to create since I first learned the wonder of words and what they could achieve on a sheet of paper. After waving my children goodbye, I began to do what I know I was born to do—write, and the ache that burrowed inside me, when I put my domestic life first, left me even as I penned my first line.

Writing is more than an art to me; it is a passion. I live and breathe along with my characters. I am at one with them when I am at my typewriter creating a life that is as real to me as my own. Their thoughts are my thoughts, their feelings are my feelings. I dig deep within myself. I must leave nothing to mere fantasy. They are me and I am them and nothing less will do.

It is as if I have a dual personality. Is it any wonder that so many great writers take to drink! You must have the strength of mind to separate the two lives you live, side by side, day after day while you are creating. You fall in love with your characters, good or evil. You empathize with them. It is the only way to write, the only way to create the reality that is necessary to fill the pages of a book. It is exhausting, fulfilling.

It is gratifying when you feel and see those pages, that began in your mind, spring to life as if by a magic power that goes beyond yourself. And it is exactly what it feels like, that the pages are writing themselves.

Since being alone, it is the only way I want to live my life. If that sounds sad, it is far from it. I have lived as a wife and mother for many years. It was satisfying and wonderful and I would not change a single moment of that precious time. Now, I am living as the writer I always craved to be, and I am loving every moment of it, even with all the discouragement that goes with being an aspiring writer, until that day finally comes when you have arrived.